The

by Hayley Lee

illustrations by Barbara Hranilovich

Harcourt Brace & Company

Orlando Atlanta Austin Boston San Francisco Chicago Dallas New York Toronto London

This is Jammal.

Jammal is big.

Jammal can jump.

Jammal can gallop.

Jammal is here
for a lesson.

I can jump.

I can gallop.

I will ride Jammal.

I'm here for a lesson.

What will happen?

Can I ride on Jammal?

Yes, I can!

Go, Jammal!